Su Wall

CHILD-INITIATED
PLAY

Hundreds of ideas for supporting
under 3s in independent play

Published 2011 by A&C Black Publishers Limited
36 Soho Square, London W1D 3QY
www.acblack.com

ISBN 978-1-4081-40529

Text © Su Wall 2011
Photographs © Sam Goodman, Fotolia, Rebecca Skerne

A CIP record for this publication is available from the British Library.

Printed in Great Britain by Latimer Trend & Company Limited

This book is produced using paper that is made from wood grown in
managed, sustainable forests. It is natural, renewable and recyclable.
The logging and manufacturing processes conform to the environmental
regulations of the country of origin.

To see our full range of titles
visit www.acblack.com

Contents

Introduction

Welcome to *Child-initiated Play* – a book dedicated to babies and children under three and to the importance of independent learning from birth.

'Child-initiated activity has many characteristics in common with play, as it is wholly decided upon by the child, based on the child's own motivation and remains under the child's control. It may involve play of many types, or it may be seen by the child as an activity with a serious purpose to explore a project or express an idea that the child may not see as pure play. It is guided by certain expectations within an Early Years setting regarding responsible use of space, time and purposes.'

(National Strategies Documentation: Learning, Playing and Interacting 2009.)

When working with the under threes, practitioners should provide a mixture of child-initiated play and focused play, through activities which are linked to the child's interests and needs in order to support and extend their learning.

Babies need more help in making their own choices because they are less experienced and practitioners need to set up the activities and take the baby to the activity, rather than the child coming to the activity. The practitioner often has to stay with the baby, introduce new opportunities, provide new materials and equipment and offer reassurance and confidence whilst role modelling in a safe and secure manner.

Activities for under threes may only last for a short period of time but they should be offered time and time again for the baby to develop the skills that will enable him to make his own choices, as he becomes more independent both physically and developmentally.

Once this occurs, the practitioner can extend the activity in terms of time and introduce additional resources and materials.

Effective Provision of Pre School Education 2004 (EPPE 2004) research showed that high quality pre-school experiences do make a difference to children and identified a number of factors that define quality including:

- highly qualified practitioners including teacher trained;
- adult-child interactions that encourage children to think deeply and express their ideas;
- practitioner's level of understanding of how children learn and an understanding of the early years curriculum;
- strong links between home and setting and finally
- an equal balance of child-initiated and adult-led learning experiences.

The best outcome for children and their learning is a mixture of child-initiated play supported by practitioners, and opportunities for learning provided and directed by practitioners.

From this research there is a clearly defined need for child-initiated learning within a high quality environment.

The role of the key person

'A key person has special responsibilities for working with a small number of children, giving them the reassurance to feel safe and cared for and building relationships with their parents.'
('Principles in to practice card 2.4 Positive Relationships: Key Person')

The role of the key person is crucial to the success of child-initiated play with the under threes. A key person will form a trusting relationship helping to ensure that the baby/child becomes confident and feels safe within the environment – without this, learning will not take place. Only when children feel confident and happy, will they thrive within the learning environment.

The key person needs to ensure that all of the child's individual needs are met and provide a suitable learning environment for them, tuning in to their needs and interests. The key person will also need to build a strong relationship with parents/carers to work together in partnership to build foundations from which babies and children can develop and reach their full potential.

A suitable environment

The environment plays a crucial role in child-initiated play. It should be well organised and attractively presented, enabling child-initiated play to occur.

The key person and their colleagues should ensure that:

- the learning environment provides a range of opportunities, both indoors and outdoors, for children to explore;

- accessible equipment is available, at the correct height and within children's sight, enabling them to choose what they want to do;

- all resources are labelled, with pictures and words, both on the container and on the shelf – where possible, stick an actual object onto the outside of the container too;

- children have access to natural materials – this could include baskets of shells, pebbles and leaves;

- cosy areas are provided for children to have quiet times.

All adults should:

- be positive role models;

- show and offer support especially when introducing a new skill or opportunity;

- have realistic and achievable expectations of the children;

- respond to the children and react to their responses;

- provide enough time to allow a child to explore the activity and to become engaged. If needed, leave the activity out, even over a couple of days if the child is still interested;

- finish an activity when the child has had enough;

- repeat activities again and again and when the child becomes confident, add to the experience by introducing new resources and extending it in a new direction;

- plan according to the individual child's interests and needs and provide opportunities and activities to extend the child's learning;

- reflect on practice, change the environment accordingly;

- ensure resources are replenished or replaced as necessary;

- provide experiences that are enjoyable and fun for both children and practitioners!

Observation, assessment and planning

In order to follow children's interests and provide opportunities for child-initiated play, the key person should observe children to find out exactly what their needs and interests are. A skilful key person will have the experience and knowledge to observe, assess and plan around an individual child. She will need to make accurate and justified observations of individual children through looking, listening and noting, and then reflecting on what the observations are telling her. From here, she can make assessments and judgements about the learning that has taken place through analysing the child's individual learning journey. Once this has been done, the key person should be able to plan the next steps for that child, focussing on their interests and needs. The key person can then plan and offer new experiences and opportunities by adapting the learning environment accordingly and empowering children to become independent learners.

Removing barriers

Practitioners need to ensure that the learning environment is safe and suitable for all of the children and that it caters for the children's own personal circumstances.

Practitioners need to:

- think about the children's needs. Have you removed all the barriers to ensure that all of the children will be able to join in the activity? There are many barriers to be considered, for example a child in a wheelchair or buggy will need chairs removed from a table to allow them access to a table top activity.

- make sure you have catered for the 'make up' of the group. Is the group predominantly made up of boys? If so, does the activity need to be taken outside as research shows boys thrive in the outdoor environment?

Have a good look at your own learning environment. Children will become more confident and more independent if all the barriers to their learning have been removed.

The outdoor environment

For young children the outdoor environment is just as important as the indoor environment. Some children prefer to be outside and learn best when the activity is outdoors. All children need access to outdoors, allowing them the fresh air, sunlight and the opportunity for exercise. With careful planning and thought, most activities can be provided both indoors and outdoors for children from birth. Always follow your policies and procedures and ensure that your children are kept safe at all times.

Taking risks

Children need to take risks in a controlled environment. Practitioners should assess and manage risk-taking carefully. Encourage children to take risks, and extend boundaries and comfort zones in order to develop their confidence and independence.

Involve parents in your risk assessments. This will lead to a shared understanding of play and risk-taking, especially in the outdoor learning environment.

Working with parents

Parents are a valuable resource and from the start can help by telling you about their child's interests, likes and dislikes. The home learning environment plays a critical role in a child's learning and can influence the development and progress a child makes.

Children's learning needs to be shared with parents. This book provides activities that can be followed up at home and suggestions as to how to develop child-initiated learning within the home environment.

What's inside this book?

Child-initiated Play explores many diverse areas of learning from messy play to mark making.

Each chapter includes:

- An introduction to the area

- Resources needed (and how to extend them)

- Getting started

- Taking it outside

- Involving parents

- A case study – an example of good practice

- Maintaining quality

- Quality checklist

- Links with early learning indicators for under 3's

With each aspect of learning, remember to use associated books and to sing nursery rhymes and songs to the children to enhance the activity. This will introduce new words and language and engage children in their learning.

Day to day events play an important part in child-initiated play and routines such as nappy time and meal times should be used as a learning opportunity and a way of helping children become more independent.

You may already be familiar with some of the core activities, but this book offers you alternatives and extensions so you can vary these key experiences for the babies and young children in your care.

Messy play

Introduction

Messy play should be part of every child's daily experience. It allows them to explore with all their senses, especially their sense of touch.
During messy play children are free to experiment and investigate imaginatively, with no right or wrong way and no need for an end product!

By providing messy play activities, you are encouraging them to explore new materials while having an enjoyable experience. Children are curious and want to find out more about the world around them and with a little thought from a practitioner, messy play is easily planned. It can be spontaneous, for example, you may have received a parcel that has shredded paper protecting the package, why not let the children carefully unpack the parcel and explore the box and the shredded paper?

Some practitioners may need help in overcoming the 'mess' that messy activities create and in addressing what is an acceptable and an unacceptable level of mess. Boundaries need to be set, followed and managed consistently; ensuring the safety of the children is adhered to at all times.

There are many reasons why children should have the opportunity to explore messy play – it clearly links to cognitive and creative development as well and personal, social and emotional development – but one of the main reasons is the hours of fun to be had!

Resources

Many messy play resources are easily found and are relatively inexpensive to buy. The early years environment has a wealth of resources that can be used for messy play, for example, mud and pebbles in the garden or dried ingredients out of the kitchen cupboards, such as flour or pasta. When deciding what opportunities to offer, think about the children's safety, for instance will the activity aggravate a child's sensitive skin? Do the stones/pebbles present a choking risk? Before any messy activity, remember to check with your policies and procedures and children's individual needs.

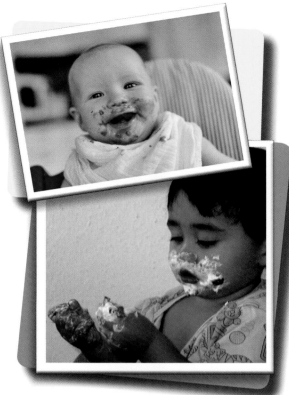

One of the first messy activities babies experience is food – when moving yoghurt around with their finger on a highchair tray they are exploring the early stages of mark making. However, there must be a balance between the child understanding that food is for eating and that this is different from messy play.

Children should have access to a good range of materials including:

- sand
- water
- dough
- cornflour and flour
- jelly
- custard
- porridge
- cooked pasta
- soil
- pebbles and stones
- shredded paper
- foam
- bubbles
- clay

Extending your resources

- Add glitter to paint, sand, water and dough
- Have a range of coloured shredded paper
- Add food colouring to cornflour, water or sand
- Add water to dry sand
- Include items with water play e.g. boats, dolls and natural items
- Add imaginary play, for example, small world farm or dinosaurs to shredded paper, cornflour or sand
- Put foam in a builder's tray
- Mix water into soil to make mud

Top tips

Put washing up liquid into paint – this will help with cleaning the paint away!

Remember messy play is fun so make sure you enjoy the fun too!

- Preparation is key to any messy activity. Children at this age will make a 'mess' and it will go everywhere but remember that this is how it should be! Clearing up materials should be at hand: baby wipes, flannels, bowl of water, soap, towels etc.
- Ensure the room is set up to encourage the children to explore the messy opportunity. Think about the activity:

- Is it visible? Is it safe? Is it accessible to all? (Get down to the child's level and see what the activity actually looks like from their perspective.)
- Does it look interesting and inviting?
- Will it interrupt any other activities that are happening at the same time?
- Do the children need protective clothing? (This shouldn't be so restrictive that it prevents the children from enjoying the activity. You may need protective clothing too!)
- Are resources at a suitable, safe height, preferably on the floor where children can easily access them?
- Have you provided a small number of tools for the children to choose from?

Water play

From birth, all children should have opportunities during their daily routine to experience water, for example, at bath time or washing their hands at various points in the day.

Children love playing with water, find it very relaxing and it is a lovely way of introducing a sensory activity to them. Experimenting and exploring water will develop children's creative ideas while having fun.

There is virtually no cost to this activity and it is very accessible to all children. However, be aware of the dangers of water and maintain supervision at all times. Always be prepared to wipe up any spillages immediately. Never leave a child during water play and check the temperature of the water – not too hot and not too cold.

Starting water play with a baby can be as basic as a bowl of water positioned on the floor for the baby to dangle their fingers or toes in. If the baby is not able to sit up on their own, support her between your legs and position the bowl on a towel directly in front of you. This activity may only last a couple of minutes but will be an enjoyable one.

Extending the water play

- Introduce a range of small containers and a large jug of water and watch as the children transfer the water from one container to another. Extend this by adding a pebble or stone to the container and let the children explore and see what happens.

- Position a water tray at a very low height and fill it with water. Have a full range of baskets nearby containing various resources for the children to choose from. The baskets could include boats, dolls, a range of empty containers, pebbles and shells for imaginary play. If the children choose the dolls for the water play, follow their interests and offer a range of baby clothes or a tea set alongside the dolls.

Taking it outside

Messy play is the perfect activity to be enjoyed outside. All of the above ideas can easily be taken outside but make sure the children are protected from the sun, wind and damp conditions.

On a warm summer's day, a paddling pool is good for keeping children's temperatures down. Offer the fun of water play in the paddling pool but be aware of how slippery it might become. You could put non-slip mats down to reduce the risk of slipping. Resources including tea sets, boats, ducks, buckets, containers can be added to the paddling pool. If a child chooses to fill a bucket, observe and watch where he takes it. Why not talk about watering the plants?

Take the children outside on a rainy day, with waterproofs and welly boots on and enjoy the experience of jumping in puddles, splashing with their feet. Extend the fun by looking at ripples in puddles made by dropping stones in or looking at the rain patterns on windows.

Put water in paint pots and let the children paint outside using paintbrushes. Extend this activity by offering a range of resources to use: different size brushes, rollers and squeegees, various printing materials including sponges and printing objects. Follow on with an actual painting activity involving paint.

Involving parents

- Share the child's experiences with parents and show how easily activities can be adapted and enjoyed at home.

- Take photographs of all kinds of messy play and show parents.

- Make up small messy play activity bags for parents to use at home – a paintbrush, a small amount of powder paint, a paint pot and some paper.

- Reinforce with parents the importance of focussing on the process of messy play rather than the end product.

- Talk to parents about making the most of bath time and opportunities to take their child swimming.

- Talk to parents about their child helping with washing up and experiencing the fun of playing with water.

Georgia, the practitioner wanted a change to the normal messy play experience for her key children aged between 10 and 14 months.

Georgia put some messy resources into four large shallow trays, one resource in each tray. She used cornflour, soapflakes, flour and sand (but you could use any other messy material you have in your setting or at home). Georgia placed the trays on the vinyl floor and put aprons on Avia, William and Miguel.

Georgia sat by the flour tray and said, 'Look what I've got! It's flour, do you want to touch it? It's dry and powdery Avia – well done for touching it.'

Georgia picked up a handful of flour and gently sprinkled it over the tray, 'Watch me sprinkle the flour.' William copied Georgia and smiled with pleasure. Miguel crawled away from the activity.

Georgia introduced the tray with cornflour and watched while Avia and William freely touched the cornflour. Avia tried to shake it off her hands and fingers and started to show signs of frustration as the cornflour stuck to her hands. Quickly, Georgia used a wipe to remove the cornflour from Avia to try to prevent her from disliking the experience.

'All gone Avia, shall we touch the sand instead?'

Georgia showed William and Avia the sand tray knowing that Avia really likes the texture of sand. Georgia watched them touch and explore the sand and enjoyed seeing how the two children showed pleasure with this material. William tried to put a handful of sand into his mouth and Georgia explained that it wouldn't taste very nice. She gently removed the sand from his hand.

Georgia took her shoes and socks off and touched the sand with her toes while Avia and William looked on. 'Shall we take your shoes and socks off too?' Georgia helped William and Avia walk in the sand, talking to them about the cool sensation on their toes.

Georgia didn't use the tray with soapflakes at all as the children clearly enjoyed the other trays.

Conclusion

This activity demonstrates how to offer a range of textures and materials for children to explore during messy play. Georgia followed the children's interest by extending the activity so that William and Avia could explore the sand with their toes as well as their fingers. She deliberately made no comment on the fact that Miguel had crawled away from the activity and showed no interest in the materials at all.

On this occasion, Georgia stuck with the materials that the children enjoyed and didn't attempt to introduce the soapflakes.

Maintaining quality

Know your children and their interests through observation and assessment and plan accordingly. With a little thought and time, it will be easy to follow and extend their learning.

Watch them carefully and look for signs of enjoyment and signs of non-enjoyment. Look out for facial expressions and hand gestures – these are good indications of how the child is feeling about the activity.

- Join in but don't direct the activity – this opportunity is for the child, follow their lead and their interests.

- Messy play is about the 'doing' and there is no right or wrong way to do it.

- Don't over clutter the activity, keep it simple and allow the children to choose what they want.

- Allow plenty of time. Don't rush the children and let them indicate when they have had enough and are ready to move on.

- Talk to the children. 'Look what's happening', 'What can you feel?', 'Does it feel cold, wet…?', 'What happens if?', 'Splash, splash!', 'Are you ready?', 'Shall we do that again?', 'What's that?'

- Offer the experience again and next time add something different to extend the activity.

Quality checklist

✓ After each session, or after each child has experienced the messy play, does it still look inviting and interesting for the next child to experience?

✓ Do we ensure that boys and girls have the same opportunity as one another?

✓ Do we share the child's experiences with parents?

✓ Do we ensure that there may not be an end product and it is the process that is key to messy play?

✓ Do we provide a full range of messy play opportunities both indoors and outdoors?

✓ Do we work as part of a team who share the same ethics about messy play?

✓ Do we share these with parents?

✓ Do we involve children in what and how they want to explore messy activities?

Links with early learning indicators for under 3s

To mess about is to play with something and it is through play – which is part of the creative process (Duffy 1998) – that children learn and develop. Children are being creative when they use materials in new ways, combine previously unconnected materials and make discoveries that are new to them, and messy play enables children to do all these things.

(Early Years Foundation Stage resources: Messy Play, Bernadette Duffy)

Personal, Social and Emotional Development

- Develops a curiosity about things and processes
- Takes pleasure in learning new skills
- Develops confidence in own abilities
- Self-confidence and self-esteem
- Social development including making relationships
- Self-control

Communication and Language

- Opportunities to express themselves through babbling and talking
- Watching and listening to others
- Learns new words and meanings

Physical Development

- Uses tools, equipment and materials
- Develops and practises fine motor control and coordination
- Body control, poise, balance

Books and Storytelling

Introduction

It's never too early to introduce books and stories to babies. From birth, babies should have the experience of sharing books with parents/carers and practitioners and begin to develop a love of books.

Books need to be available everywhere, both indoors and outdoors and storytime must be part of the daily routine with plenty of opportunities for a spontaneous story to take place during the day.

Reading a story is a great way of communicating with babies and should be an interesting and rewarding experience for both you and the baby.

Introducing rhymes and rhyming books from an early age will help to develop an awareness of rhyme and rhythm within young children's speech. There are plenty of rhyming board books available for you to choose from.

Try to maximise the opportunities during the day to tell a story without the use of an actual book. Tell a story about the events of the day, what has happened and what might happen next.

There should be opportunities for children to choose their own books and they should have a special place within your setting where they can sit and look at the book by themselves. A range of big books is ideal for reading with a small group of children – the whole group should be able to see both the pictures and the print easily.

Resources

Books are an essential resource within every environment and babies must have the opportunity to access them. Although they can be expensive, if looked after properly with care and love, they will last for many years.

Within many communities, there are local libraries and/or mobile libraries where you can access a range of books free of charge with no cost to you or your families. Using libraries is a great way of varying the range of books you have on offer.

Children should have access to:

- Board books
- Cloth books
- Factual books – books with pictures of real objects and people
- Pop-up books
- Flap-books
- Books with no print
- Books with print
- Big books
- A wide range of storybooks

Extending your resources

- Use a story aid e.g. a hand puppet
- Use a story sack (you can make your own!)
- Use story CDs
- Use a visual aid during the story, for example, a teddy bear or a doll
- Have props available e.g. a range of hats
- Listen to music associated with the story
- Link a favourite nursery rhyme/song to the story
- Have pens and paper available for children to illustrate their own stories

Top tip

It's never too early to start reading to babies and sharing a love of books.

Getting started

- Before you start any storytime remember to be prepared. Look at the book before you begin and familiarise yourself with the layout, the text and the pictures, ensuring that you are confident to use the book in front of the children and sometimes in front of other professionals and parents too.

- Remove any books that display negative images that might influence children in a negative way e.g. books with fighting in.

- Think about the children, their age and understanding and ensure books are appropriate for them.

- Have any props or story aids easily at hand.

- Books need to be available for children to access by themselves. Provide books in a book basket in a quiet area.

- Ensure that the room is set up to encourage the children to explore books. Think about the book area:

  - Is it visible?

  - Is it a quiet area?

  - Is it accessible to all?

  - Does it look interesting and inviting?

  - Are there too many/not enough books?

  - Does it have comfortable soft cushions and furnishing?

  - Will storytime be interrupted by any other activities that are happening at the same time?

Making your own books

Making your own books for babies and young children is a fun and exciting way of bringing books to life. It's very rewarding and can be an inexpensive activity. With a little time, thought and creativity, you can make a wide range of exciting books for your book area.

Zig-zag books

From a very young age babies respond to contrasting colours. Use black and white card cut into various shapes. Stick the black shapes on to the white card and the white shapes on to the black card. If you have access to a laminator, laminate the pages, hole punch them and tie them together using ribbon or wool.

'My family' books

Children love to see themselves in books. Ask parents to bring in a selection of photos of their child and family. You could buy disposable cameras and give each family a camera to take home and use.

Stick the photos on to card or put them in a small album and write the names of family members underneath. If you have access to a laminator, laminate the pages, hole punch them and tie them together using ribbon or wool. You could staple the pages together, but make sure you cover the staples with sticky tape so that they don't scratch the child.

You could make a similar book about 'Our day'. Take a range of photos of children at different times during a normal day and make them into a book with captions.

'Where is teddy today?' book

Take a favourite teddy bear out into the local community and photograph him in various places. This could include: teddy in a trolley at the local supermarket, at the bus stop, on the swings, at the library, feeding the ducks, up a tree and so on. Print out the photos, stick on to card and write underneath what teddy is doing. If you have access to a laminator, laminate the pages, hole punch them and tie them together using ribbon or wool.

Our pictures

Let the children paint, stick or mark make. On each picture write the child's name and photograph each picture. With an older child, if they have told you what the picture is, write this too. Remember not to ask the child what their picture is. In their eyes it is clear what they have made!

Our holiday adventure

When a child goes on holiday, let them borrow a teddy bear or a 'holiday doll' and a disposable camera. Ask the parents to take photos of the child with the toy. This could be a picture of the child and the toy on an aeroplane or on the beach. Print them out, stick them on to card and write underneath where the toy has been and what it has been doing. You could tie or staple the pages together.

A favourite song

Use either clip art on a computer or carefully chosen wrapping paper to make a song book such as 'Five Little Ducks'. Cut out fifteen ducks and one mummy duck. Laminate the ducks, one duck on the first page, two ducks on the second page right through to five ducks on the last page. Hole punch the laminated pages and tie together using ribbon or wool. For the mummy duck, laminate and stick on to a lollipop stick. Use the book whilst singing the song.

Taking it outside

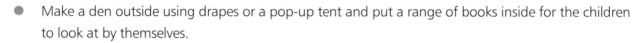

Reading books and storytelling are perfect activities to be enjoyed outside. All of the above ideas can easily be taken outside but make sure the children are protected from the sun, wind and damp conditions. Be aware of insects and other wildlife in the garden especially with babies and young children who are less mobile. Here are some ideas:

- Make a den outside using drapes or a pop-up tent and put a range of books inside for the children to look at by themselves.

- On a warm day, in a quiet area, sit together on a bench or a rug and enjoy your story time together. Put the books in a basket and let the children choose.

- Read books associated with outdoors such as 'We're going on a bear hunt' by Michael Rosen and Helen Oxenbury.

- Tell your own story about what's happening outside and use the natural resources around you to enhance your story.

Involving parents

- Share the child's experiences with parents and emphasise the importance of books at home.

- Start a book library encouraging parents to borrow books to share with their child.

- Display suitable books for children which parents can look at and get ideas from.

- Encourage parents to bring in favourite story books from home.

- Share information with parents about local libraries and the Bookstart project.

- Display times and dates of local community activities e.g. 'storytime' at the library.

- Encourage parents to bring in photos of their family and community for you to make into a book.

Sam, aged 20 months, arrived at his childminder's with the book 'Dear Zoo' by Rod Campbell. Sam's dad spoke to the childminder Ali, explaining to her that Sam was taking this book everywhere with him and that it was currently his favourite book. Ali thanked Sam's dad for bringing the book in and took Sam with his book to the book area.

The book area was located in a quiet cosy corner of the room with lots of soft furnishings and a number of baskets on the floor, containing a range of books including cloth, board, factual and story books.

Sam sat on Ali's lap.

'Let's have a look at your book Sam, what's inside?'

Ali encouraged Sam to explore the book by turning the pages and opening the flaps.

'Look Sam, it's a monkey and he's eating a banana.'

Ali imitated the noise and movement of a monkey. Sam copied him with laughter and delight.

Pascal, a friend of Sam's, walked over to the book area. Sam pointed to the book and Ali said, 'Sam, show Pascal where the monkey is.' Both boys looked at the book and started laughing at each other.

Ali continued with the book and at the end handed the boys a closed basket and said,

'Look, what's inside the basket?'

Both boys opened the lid and pulled out a range of animal puppets that Ali had loaned from the local toy library. Spontaneously, they put a puppet on each hand and imitated the noises of the animals.

Ali started to sing the first of several nursery rhymes including: Down in the Jungle, Five Little Monkeys, Five Speckled Frogs, Elephants go like this and that, Daddy's taking us to the Zoo tomorrow.

Sam and Pascal joined in by clapping and dancing. Ali picked up Sam's book and asked him if he would put it on the interest table. Sam nodded and returned to looking at the hand puppets. Ali moved away from the book area and observed the boys from a distance.

Later that day, Ali ensured that she had signed permission from the parents, and took both children to the local library for story time.

Ali shared the experiences with both boys' parents and how they had enjoyed the story time, both in the home and at the library.

Conclusion

This case study clearly demonstrates a childminder following a child's interest that has originated at home, making a clear partnership between home and the childminder for the benefit of Sam.

Sam clearly enjoys books and stories and enjoyed sharing his book with Pascal. Ali introduced new words and rhymes through singing a range of songs and the following day used the local community amenities to extend the learning by visiting the local library.

Finally, Ali used her skills well to remove herself from the book area and provide opportunities for Sam to explore the books and puppets by himself and with his friend Pascal.

Maintaining quality

- Provide an inviting book area, with plenty of soft cushions, rugs and soft furnishings with a wide selection of books for children and practitioners to access.

- During story time, sit with the children at their level, limit the size of the group and make sure the children can see the book with ease.

- Read the text slowly, allowing plenty of time for each page and for the children to look at the pictures.

- Use plenty of facial expression and voice tone to emphasise key words and encourage the children to touch and feel the books for themselves.

- Know your children and their interests through observation and assessment. With a little thought and time, it will be easy to follow and extend their development by introducing books linked to their interests.

- Watch the children carefully for signs of enjoyment and signs of non-enjoyment. Look out for facial expressions and hand gestures – these are good indicators of how the child is feeling.

- After each session or after each child has 'experienced' the book area, does it still look inviting and interesting for the next child to experience?

- Books from other cultures need to be visible, encouraging children, parents and practitioners to view other cultures and communities positively.

- Provide opportunities for children to choose their own books and to look at the books by themselves. Join in but don't direct. This opportunity is for the child, follow their lead and their interests.

- Allow plenty of time. Don't rush the children and let them decide when they have had enough and are ready to move on.

- Talk to the children by saying things like 'What book shall we have?', 'Let's turn the page', 'Did you enjoy that?', 'Are you ready?', 'Shall we do that again?'

- Offer the experience again. Keep reading the same stories over and over again and next time add something different e.g. a hand puppet to extend the activity.

- Make your own books!

Role-play

Role-play starts at a very early age with simple activities such as wearing different hats and shoes or playing with sock puppets or a tea set. Through role-play, children have the chance to learn about real life experiences in a safe and secure environment. It provides an opportunity to deal with issues that may be sensitive and can be used to present positive images portraying gender, culture and disability.

You can also include ICT in any role-play area. It reflects children's day-to-day experiences by offering such things as mobile phones, computers and laptops that the children can relate back to their home environment.

Role-play is the perfect activity for engaging children in mark making and the use of environmental print. With any aspect of role-play, mark making can easily be included e.g. making a shopping list or sending and posting a letter at the post office.

Most of all, children will have so much fun and enjoyment within the role-play area!

Resources

There are many resources readily available that can be used for role-play.

These might include:

- A tea set – cups, teapot, jug, and cutlery
- Dressing up clothes (make sure these are easy for young children to put on and take off)
- A variety of hats and shoes
- Child-size vacuum cleaner, dustpan and brush
- A range of materials and drapes
- Dolls, pushchairs, bottles and clothes
- Mirrors (ensure they are safe for children to use)
- Receipts, bus tickets and magazines
- A range of mark making materials – old diaries, telephone books, note pads, a selection of crayons, pens and envelopes

Top tip

Before you throw anything anyway, ask yourself, can it be used for role-play?

Extending your resources

With the under threes, children don't necessarily need a role-play area – just props or a basket containing hats, bags and other objects will present many opportunities.

For very young babies, familiar objects such as brushes, feeding bowls and baby bottles are perfect resources to use with dolls.

Making your own resources for babies and children is a great way of bringing role-play to life. With a little time, thought and creativity, you can make a wide range of exciting items for your role-play area. Here are some suggestions:

- Add pretend food to a tea set. Use a basic dough recipe. Mix flour, salt and water to make dough shapes with children, and then slowly bake till hard, paint and decorate.
- Use tablecloths and 'invite' teddy bears to have a teddy bear's picnic.
- Collect empty boxes from your local supermarket and use them in your role-play area. They can be used as a table for your tea set, a washing machine for the kitchen, or cover with a drape for a den.
- Make your own hats.
- Position recipe cards and cookery magazines next to bowls and spoons.
- Include an airer and some pegs with dolls' clothes.
- Visit your local amenities and adapt your role-play area to coincide with your visits.
- Include relevant books.

Getting started

- Avoid any resources that display negative images that would influence children's learning e.g. plastic guns.

- Think about the children, their age and level of understanding, and ensure resources are appropriate.

- Have a range of suitable books associated with role-play in a basket, showing positive images to extend children's learning.

- Resources need to be suitable for the very young. Be aware of health and safety and follow your policies and procedures, especially with jewellery, scarves and belts.

- Role-play resources need to be available for children to access by themselves e.g. place dressing up clothes in a quiet area.

- Watch the children carefully and look for signs of enjoyment and signs of non-enjoyment. Look out for facial expressions and hand gestures – these are good indications as to how the child is feeling.

- Provide role-play outdoors too.

- Ensure the room is set up to encourage children to explore and enjoy the role-play area. Think about the positioning of the area:

  - Is it visible?

  - Is it a quiet area?

  - Is it accessible to all?

  - Does it look interesting and inviting?

  - Will role-play be interrupted by any other activities that are happening at the same time?

  - Is there enough space?

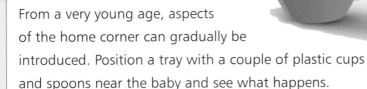

The home corner

From a very young age, aspects of the home corner can gradually be introduced. Position a tray with a couple of plastic cups and spoons near the baby and see what happens.

As the baby becomes more confident, include a teapot, a jug and a small bowl. Have a basket nearby to encourage the child to choose other items such as plates, bowls and food. Following the children's interests, add a blanket and a teddy bear and have a teddy bear's picnic.

Leading on from this, as the child becomes older and shows an interest in food, why not introduce a very simple cooking activity? Let the child make some sandwiches and choose which fillings to use. This will encourage good hand-eye coordination as well as opportunities for choice. Extend this by making a shopping list and then visiting a local supermarket to buy the bread and fillings. Remember with any cooking activity or trip, follow your own policies and procedures ensuring the safety of the children at all times.

Use a trolley or basket to store various home corner items in and watch to see which items are chosen for investigation. Have a range of dolls and accessories including, bottles, bibs, clothes, shoes, hats, pushchairs, towels and blankets in the trolley. Extend this by putting these items near the water tray for doll's bath time or washing the doll's clothes.

Other ideas for the trolley:

- spoons, saucepans, colanders, chopping boards, sieves, empty washed out bottles and containers

- envelopes, pencils, receipts, old diaries, rulers, children's scissors, pads of various paper and card

- hats, shoes, bags, clothes, drapes, large necklaces, coats and gloves

Follow the children's interest and extend whenever possible. Children love to dress up and love to wear your shoes and your hats!

Taking it outside

You can take any aspect of role-play outside. A teddy bear's picnic is perfect for taking outside. Make sure children are protected from the sun, wind and damp conditions. Provide welly boots, waterproofs, umbrellas and hats for children to wear outside. This is role-play in itself.

Be aware of insects and other wildlife in the garden especially with very young babies.

Some further ideas:

- After it rains, put welly boots on. Go outside, splash in puddles and experience wet muddy days.

- Make a den outside using drapes or a pop-up tent and put a range of resources inside for the children to explore by themselves. The next day add another item to the tent/den.

- Collect large empty boxes from supermarkets and use them to make a train, a bus, a builder's yard or a house outside.

Involving parents

- Share the child's experiences with their parents and show how easily role-play can be enjoyed within the home environment.

- Ask parents to bring in items that could be used in a role-play area.

- Provide ideas for parents to try at home with their children such as helping with the gardening, washing up, shopping, dressing up and the process of 'post and letters'.

- Take photos of children in the role-play area and display for parents to see.

- Make small role-play bags to lend to parents to use at home.

Bhavin who is two has recently started nursery, two afternoons a week, since moving with his parents as an asylum seeker family. Bhavin has been reluctant to communicate verbally and English is his second language. The nursery is trying new techniques to welcome Bhavin's parents and to share his learning and interests with them.

On arrival, Bhavin always goes straight to the home corner, away from the other children and plays with the cooker by himself. He is contented to stay there for the full afternoon, with little or no contact with his peers or practitioners.

Bhavin's key worker, Cathy, ensures that the home corner is available for Bhavin to access and is set up in the same way every day while Bhavin becomes familiar and confident with the nursery environment.

Cathy observes Bhavin playing with the pretend food alongside Zara who is just over two. Cathy instigates a cooking activity. She goes and sits in the home corner near to Bhavin with flour, water, a bowl and utensils including a rolling pin and some pastry cutters.

'Zara, shall we make some food for the home corner?' Zara agrees and together they mix a basic dough recipe. While making the dough, Cathy involves Bhavin by sharing the processes verbally with him.

Zara makes pretend biscuits with the dough and Cathy passes Bhavin a small amount of dough and shows him how to roll it using the rolling pin.

'Bhavin, look what happens to the dough, shall we roll it out? Good boy Bhavin, that's right. Well done!' Bhavin smiles at Cathy and she passes him more dough. Cathy takes photographs of Bhavin.

The process is repeated and Cathy bakes the dough slowly in a warm oven over night.

The following afternoon, Cathy shows Bhavin his pretend food and together they place the food in the home corner.

Cathy prints the photos and makes a book for Bhavin and his family to share, showing the fun Bhavin had making the food. At story time, Cathy shared the book with Bhavin and his friends.

Conclusion

This is a good example of a practitioner taking the learning to the child where he feels most comfortable. Cathy extended the activity by the use of a camera and making a personalised book of the process through photos.

This was an excellent way of communicating with Bhavin and also communicating with his family, enabling Cathy to share the experiences and the learning with them in a positive way.

Maintaining quality

- Work alongside children, being a role model, providing positive images and showing them how to use the resources.

- During role-play, limit the size of the group and make sure all the children can follow their own interests and preferences.

- Use suitable language and support children in the use of their vocabulary. Introduce new words when appropriate and allow time for children to respond. Listen carefully and use plenty of praise and encouragement.

- Know when to join in, when to stand back and when to interact through asking questions and offering suggestions to support their play and learning.

- Have a balance between adult-led and child-led opportunities.

- Provide opportunities for children to find out for themselves. Allow them to experiment and share their experiences.

- Organise visitors or trips to extend your role-play e.g. invite your local policeman or post lady to meet the children and/or visit the local café or fire station.

- Be aware, some children may not enjoy certain aspects of role-play e.g. dressing up. Respect and understand their likes and dislikes and what they are comfortable doing.

- Recognise the importance of cultural and gender differences and reflect this in the practice.

- Use environmental print to label items within the area.

- After each session or after each child has experienced the role-play area, does it still look inviting and interesting for the next child to experience?

- Most of all, join in and have fun yourself!

Quality checklist

✔ Do we change our role-play area often enough?

✔ Is role-play available both indoors and outdoors?

✔ Does our role-play area reflect the community within the area?

✔ Do practitioners join in and be a positive role model?

✔ Do we ensure that boys and girls have the same opportunities?

Links with early
learning indicators
for under 3s

Recognising the importance of being able to think creatively and imaginatively is key to understanding how young children begin to make a sense of the work around them and create links in to their learning.

(Planning for Children's Play and Learning Drake 2009)

Personal, Social and Emotional Development

- Takes pleasure in learning new skills
- Develops confidence in own abilities
- Self-confidence and self-esteem
- Social development including making relationships

Communication and Language

- Begins to develop language
- Express themselves through babbling and talking
- Watching and listening to others
- Learns new words and meanings
- Explores and experiments with sounds and words

Physical Development

- Using tools, equipment and materials
- Develop and practise fine motor control and coordination
- Express themselves through action and sounds
- Begin to make, manipulate objects and tools

Creativity

All children should have opportunities to be creative in paint, clay, construction, collage, music, singing and dancing. Children need to feel secure and confident in order for them to become creative and this begins with good attachment and by having stable relationships. Creativity enhances children's self esteem and achievement as the emphasis is very much on the process rather than the end product. There is no right or wrong way of being creative but children should have the freedom to experiment and explore with a variety of textures, materials and resources.

Creativity can be messy so clear boundaries should be set and followed as to what is an acceptable level of mess and what is not. Practitioners must bear this in mind and allow children to explore, create their own works of art and have the freedom to be imaginative. However, some children may not have the confidence to be creative so take it at the children's individual pace and follow their needs and interests.

- Work sensitively with children as your role is crucial in encouraging creativity to take place.

- Know your children and their interests through observation and assessment and plan accordingly. With a little thought and time, it will be easy to follow and extend their interests.

- Show the children how to use resources and help them to become familiar and confident with them.

- Provide opportunities for children's specific religious or cultural beliefs.

- Watch the children carefully and look for signs of enjoyment and signs of non-enjoyment. Look out for facial expressions and hand gestures – these are good indications as to how the child is feeling about the activity.

- Join in but don't direct the activity, this opportunity is for the child – follow their lead and their interests.

- Creativity is about the 'doing'. There is no right or wrong way to do this so make sure creative opportunities are accessible to all.

- Don't over clutter the activity. Keep it simple and allow for children to choose what they need.

- Allow plenty of time. Don't rush the children and let them dictate when they have had enough and are ready to move on.

- Place resources on the floor, on mats, for children to access and remove chairs from tables so they can more easily move from one activity to another.

- Offer opportunities to work on small and large scale creations. See 'The Little Book of Big Projects' (A & C Black/Featherstone) for more ideas.

- After each session, does the area still look inviting and interesting for the next child to experience?

- Where possible, encourage artists to come and work alongside children.

- Offer the experience again and next time add something different to extend the activity.

Quality checklist

✓ Do we value each child's own creative skills?

✓ Do we focus on the process rather than the end product?

✓ Do we think of creativity in its wider context – for example the natural world, exploring patterns in mud and making dens?

✓ Do we ensure the child is confident and comfortable in the environment to allow for their creativity to take place?

✓ Do we work with parents to show the importance of valuing creativity?

✓ Do we lead by example?

✓ Do we provide a wide range of materials and opportunities?

43

Links with early learning indicators for under 3s

Children's creativity must be extended by the provision of support for their curiosity, exploration and play. They must be provided with opportunities to explore and share their thoughts, ideas and feelings for example, through a variety of art, music, movement, dance, imaginative and role play activities, mathematics and design and technology.

(Practice Guidance for the Early Years Foundation Stage)

Personal, Social and Emotional Development

- Develops a curiosity about things and processes
- Takes pleasure in learning new skills
- Develops confidence in own abilities
- Self-confidence and self-esteem
- Social development including making relationships
- Self-control

Communication and Language

- Express themselves through babbling and talking
- Watching and listening to others
- Learns new words and meanings

Physical Development

- Uses tools, equipment and materials
- Develops and practises fine motor control and coordination
- Body control, poise, balance

Making music

Introduction

Children are influenced by music in all shapes and forms and should have daily opportunities to sing and make music. There are many aspects to music: hearing, listening, dancing, singing and with older children, actually making an instrument. Research shows that even a foetus can hear the music the mother is hearing and a new born baby will respond positively to the sounds within the immediate environment.

Music often starts with singing to babies – singing lullabies whilst gently rocking the baby. Practitioners need to be confident with singing and combined with holding a baby close it's a great way of forming good attachment.

Music is a form of communication and is a way of expressing many different types of emotions. Music can help babies relax and sleep. Providing the right music is played it can have a calming affect. You can introduce rhythm to babies through music which is an essential skill for speaking, listening and reading. Children instinctively move to music and this in turn develops their balance, co-ordination, body awareness and rhythm.

With babies and very young children, there is often no right or wrong way of experimenting with music. It is an excellent opportunity for children to express themselves and to communicate with peers and practitioners.

Music is great fun! Babies and children love to make plenty of noise with instruments and love to dance and move to music.

45

Resources

A good set of musical instruments can be very expensive but it's definitely worth investing in good quality wooden instruments that will last for years. Instruments should represent all cultures from around the world. For babies and young children, concentrate on percussion instruments, and preferably those that encourage the use of both hands.

A good range of instruments include:

- wrist and ankle bells
- xylophones
- tambourines
- drums
- rainmakers
- shakers

There are many opportunities within the environment to create your own music using:

- saucepans
- wooden and metal spoons
- two bricks
- empty plastic bottles filled with pasta and then sealed
- sandpaper blocks
- chopsticks
- empty plastic washing up bowls and buckets

Extending your resources

- Add ribbons and streamers.
- Include various fabrics and materials for dancing.
- Use a nursery rhyme book and sing your way. through the book with the children.
- Play instruments while singing.
- Investigate and explore old CD players.
- Provide a good range of CDs representing all aspects of rhythm, tempo, cultures, poems and rhymes.

Top tip

Don't forget you can make music out of virtually anything!

Getting started

Very young babies

- With very young babies, the starting point is as simple as laying the baby on a mat and gently tapping various musical instruments for her to hear and see.

- Gently fasten bells or ribbons to her wrists or ankles so she can make her own music too.

As babies develop

- Place a basket of instruments on a carpeted area with soft cushions for the babies to access.

- Ensure there are enough instruments for all the children to play at the same time.

- Ensure the room is set up to encourage the children to explore the opportunity. Think about the positioning of the activity:

  - Is it visible?

  - Is it accessible to all?

  - Does it look interesting and inviting?

  - Will it interrupt any other activities that are happening at the same time?

- Ensure that the range of instruments represents music from around the world.

- Have plenty of space for dancing and movement to happen.

- Teach older children how to use CD players.

Be creative

Making your own music for children is a fun and exciting way of bringing music to life. It is very rewarding and can be an inexpensive activity.

Shakers

Collect some plastic bottles of all different shapes and sizes. Wash the bottles and their tops thoroughly. Using a range of materials such as pebbles, feathers and dried pasta, fill the bottles with one material up to half full. Glue the tops securely to the bottles and allow to dry.

Drums

Collect a range of empty boxes. Cover the opening of the box with greaseproof paper and use an elastic band to secure the paper across the opening. To create different sounds, tighten and loosen the greaseproof paper. Decorate the box as desired. Use either hands, fingers or a tapping stick to make different noises.

Taking it outside

All of the ideas can easily be taken outside but make sure the children are protected from the sun, wind and damp conditions.

Being outside provides children with the freedom to play instruments loudly and to sing and dance as noisily as they want to!

Some further ideas:

- Tie some saucepans to an old clothes airer and provide a range of wooden and metal spoons for the children to make music with.

- Go on a 'music hunt' around the environment. Listen out for natural sounds including birds singing, grasses swaying in the wind and wind chimes.

- Go on a 'music-making hunt' around the environment. Give the children a beater to tap different objects with and listen to the sounds being made. You could suggest they try rubbing the beater up and down a tree.

- Sing action songs outside and do the actions with the children. Try 'The Grand Old Duke of York', 'I am the music man', 'Ring o-ring of roses', 'I can play on the big bass drum'.

- Take a battery-powered CD player outside. Provide dressing up clothes to dance in, and musical instruments, streamers and ribbons to dance with.

Involving parents

- Share the child's experiences with parents and show how easy activities can be adapted and enjoyed at home.

- Share with parents the importance of songs and rhymes in children's language development.

- Ask parents if they are artists or musicians and see if they will come and share their skills with the children.

- Reinforce the importance of using appropriate and varied music with their children.

- Make music bags for parents to take home and use – a CD, some streamers and bells.

Milly is nine months old and has shown a great interest in music since starting nursery. Whenever music is played, Milly immediately turns to the music and gently rocks to the beat of the sounds.

Jack, the practitioner has spoken to her parents and has discovered that Milly's dad, Trevor is a musician who plays the bongos and that mum Emma, loves to dance and always has music playing in the house.

On a carpeted area, Jack arranged some cushions, a CD player with a selection of CDs and a box full of musical instruments. Jack made sure that the area was away from the quiet area to ensure the noise didn't disturb other babies who were trying to rest.

Jack chose a number of suitable instruments for Milly and her two friends including a rainmaker, bells and a shaker. Jack played an appropriate CD and watched Milly moving and swaying to the tunes. Jack carefully stood Milly up and supported her on her legs encouraging Milly to dance.

'Milly, shall we make some music?'

Jack carefully watched Milly crawl over and sit next to the box of instruments. She looked into the box and touched the instruments with delight on her face. Out of sight, Jack picked up the rainmaker and gently shook it behind his back.

'Listen Milly, what's that you can hear?' Jack showed Milly the instrument and how to make the sound. 'Milly can you hear the rainmaker? Do you want to shake it Milly?'

Jack passed Milly a rainmaker and together they shook the instruments.

'Well done Milly.' Milly pulled out some bells and shook them. Jack said, 'Look, you have the bells, listen to the sound they make.'

Chloe and Shavina crawled over to the box and picked the bells too. Jack maintained close supervision to ensure that the three babies didn't hit each other with the instruments.

Jack gently sang lullabies to the babies while they remained interested in the music.

At the end of the day, Jack spoke to Milly parents about music and Trevor agreed to come in to the baby unit and to play his bongos, sharing his experience and love of music with the babies.

Conclusion

Although this activity only lasted a few minutes, Jack clearly followed Milly's interest by providing a range of instruments and sounds. Jack nurtured Milly's curiosity by providing a box of instruments and by making sounds out of sight and waiting for a response from Milly.

Milly clearly showed signs of movement which Jack followed by providing the opportunity for Milly to stand up and dance.

Using parental partnership, Jack was able to extend the activity by introducing a new instrument and some Caribbean music for the babies to experience.

Maintaining quality

- Ensure there are times in the day that are specifically for music time.

- Restrict the volume level of the music being played and avoid having music playing all day as 'background' noise.

- Ensure the range of CDs is appropriate and check the lyrics of pop songs.

- Work sensitively with children as your role is crucial in encouraging expression through music.

- Place resources on the floor, on mats, for children to access. Remove chairs from tables so children are not restricted.

- Show the children how to use instruments and help them become familiar and confident with them.

- Provide opportunities for children's specific religious or cultural beliefs with their musical customs.

- Watch the children carefully and watch for signs of enjoyment and signs of non-enjoyment. Look out for facial expressions and hand gestures. These are good indications of how the child is feeling about the activity.

- Join in but don't be tempted to direct the activity – this opportunity is for the child so follow their lead and their interests.

- Creating music is about the doing and there is no right or wrong way to do this so musical activities should be accessible to all.

- Where possible, encourage musicians from the local community to come and work alongside children. Ask if any parents play instruments and invite them in to share their music with the children.

Quality checklist

✓ Do we value music and provide plenty of opportunities?

✓ Is there enough space to allow the children to be musical without disturbing other children?

✓ Do we invite musicians into the setting to play to the children?

✓ Do we have a full range of musical instruments?

✓ Do we lead by example and show children how to use and care for musical instruments?

✓ Do we use everyday objects to make sounds and music?

Links with early learning indicators for under 3s

Give opportunities for children to work alongside artists and other creative adults to that they can see first hand different ways of expressing and communicating ideas to different responses to media and materials. (Practice Guidance for the Early Years Foundation Stage)

Personal, Social and Emotional Development

- Develops a curiosity about things and processes
- Takes pleasure in learning new skills
- Develops confidence in own abilities
- Self-confidence and self-esteem
- Social development including making relationships
- Self-control

Communication and Language

- Express themselves through babbling and talking
- Watching and listening to others
- Learns new words and meanings
- Listens to and enjoys rhythmic patterns

Physical Development

- Using tools, equipment and materials
- Develop and practice fine motor control and coordination
- Body control, poise, balance

Outdoor play

Introduction

All children need access to the outdoor environment. Some children learn best and are more focussed when they are outside. The outdoor environment is just as important as the indoor environment and they should compliment each other. Children from birth need fresh air, daylight and exercise and with the correct clothes, children and practitioners can go outside in all weathers, except for a foggy day or periods of intense cold. Children have very sensitive skins, so sun cream and hats should be used in the summer months and plenty of layers, waterproof outfits and welly boots should be worn during autumn and winter.

Children should be provided with many opportunities when they are outside, for example, allowing them to take risks through climbing and balancing and to use large motor skills for running and jumping.

In today's society, many children don't have access to an outdoor environment so it's vital that they are provided with outdoor play on a daily basis – free flow from indoor to outdoor where possible.

53

Resources

Outdoor resources can be very expensive to buy but it is definitely worth investing in a number of high quality pieces of equipment. These will last for years and children will use them time and time again.

These might include:

- Trucks
- Cart
- Wheelbarrows
- Blocks
- 'A' frames
- Barrels
- Balls
- Hoops
- Bats
- Bikes
- Planks
- Crates, cardboard tubes
- Guttering and drainpipes
- Buckets, bowls and boxes

However, there are other items that can be easily collected to use outdoors with very little cost:

- Cardboard boxes – all sizes
- Empty containers
- Drapes and fabrics
- Sticks and stones
- Mark making tools
- Tyres and milk crates

Top tip

Practitioners need suitable clothing too as well as the children when enjoying the outdoor environment.

Extending your resources

- Put small world animals, dinosaurs or cars into cardboard boxes for children to play with outside
- Drape fabric over an 'A' frame or washing line.
- Make a tent and have a basket full of books and some torches inside.
- Play music outdoors.
- Provide laundry baskets with clothes or a tea set.
- Encourage children to use their senses. Listen out for noises from aeroplanes, cars, birds and smell and touch flowers and shrubs.

- At the beginning of the day, check the outdoor environment and remove any unwanted or broken items. Make sure that wooden resources are splinter free and safe for children to use.

- Ensure there are plenty of appropriate resources for all the children to access.

- Provide suitable clothing to protect children from all types of weather.

- Position the equipment in a safe place and ensure there is plenty of safe room around just in case a child falls.

- Ensure the outdoor space is set up invitingly to encourage the children to explore and be excited. Think about the positioning of the resources:

  - Are they visible?

  - Are they accessible to all?

  - Do they look interesting and inviting?

  - Will the activity interrupt any other activities that are happening at the same time?

- Get down to the child's level and see what the activity actually looks like from their perspective.

- Make sure the outdoor environment is not over crowded with too many resources.

Seasonal walks

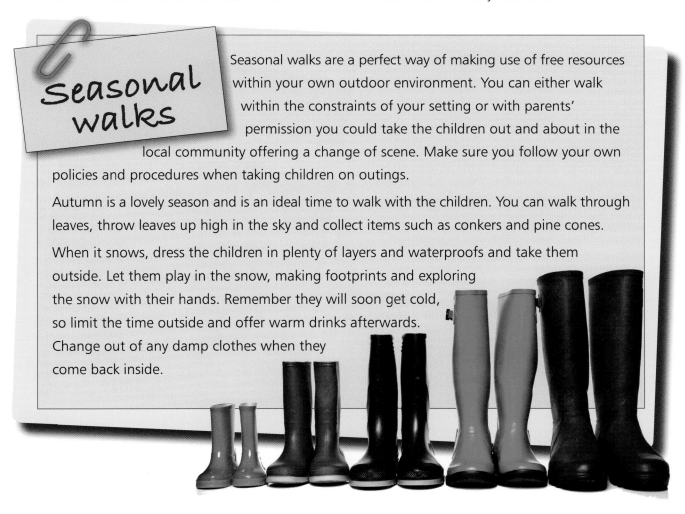

Seasonal walks are a perfect way of making use of free resources within your own outdoor environment. You can either walk within the constraints of your setting or with parents' permission you could take the children out and about in the local community offering a change of scene. Make sure you follow your own policies and procedures when taking children on outings.

Autumn is a lovely season and is an ideal time to walk with the children. You can walk through leaves, throw leaves up high in the sky and collect items such as conkers and pine cones.

When it snows, dress the children in plenty of layers and waterproofs and take them outside. Let them play in the snow, making footprints and exploring the snow with their hands. Remember they will soon get cold, so limit the time outside and offer warm drinks afterwards. Change out of any damp clothes when they come back inside.

Gardening

Gardening is a great experience for children of all ages. It's easy to do and encourages children to care and look after plants while learning about the cycle of growth. Gardening can be as simple as providing a muddy area with a wheelbarrow and some gardening tools and watching what happens next.

Use pots, baskets or grow bags to grow spring flowers such as daffodils, tulips or crocuses. Grow your own vegetables in a vegetable plot. Start off small with easy to grow vegetables such as peas and tomatoes. Children will enjoy watering the vegetables using watering cans. Extend the vegetable growing by taking them into the kitchen and cooking with them. Vegetable soup is easy to make and even very young children can help with the chopping of the ingredients.

Defined areas

The outdoor environment needs to have defined areas for children. They can be large or small but you need to think about how the areas can work well together e.g. positioning a blanket with a basket of books needs to be in a quiet corner of the garden away from the busy area of bikes and trikes.

Defined areas could include:

- Role-play area
- Mark making area
- Book area
- Creative area
- Messy area
- Construction area

Taking it inside!

With thought and planning, many of the outdoor activities and smaller resources can be taken and used *inside*. Consideration must be given to the safety of the children and resources, especially with the larger equipment. Follow your own policies and procedures and ensure risks assessments have been completed.

Some further ideas:

- Bring natural items inside and place them in an empty water tray or display them on a table. This can include twigs, leaves, conkers and actual snow.

- Make a den using drapes or a pop up tent and put a range of resources inside e.g. small world animals or books for the children to explore by themselves.

- Have a picnic lunch or a teddy bear's picnic on a rug.

- Clear away tables and chairs and bring trikes or bats and balls inside.

- Clear a space and lay blankets and mats down for the babies to crawl on, roll on and move freely around.

Involving parents

- Share the child's experiences with parents.

- Ask parents to help you with the gardening, especially if you have a large vegetable plot.

- Take photographs and display for parents to see.

- Share the importance of outdoor play with parents and encourage them to use their local parks and amenities.

- Encourage parents to provide suitable clothing and protection for outdoor play.

Case study

Anu is a practitioner working within a small baby room. Unfortunately, the nursery is set in an old Victorian building where the under 12 months are situated upstairs with no access to free flow indoors and outdoors.

Anu is very aware that the babies need to go outside daily and uses the support of the manager to help with transporting babies up and down the stairs.

Before the babies arrive, Anu set up the outdoor environment by hanging a couple of mobiles and wind chimes on the trees and attaching ribbon and streamers to the bottom branches for the babies to reach and touch. Anu placed a travel rug with a waterproof lining under a tree and then put an activity mat on top with cushions and soft furnishing around. Anu took a range of baskets outside containing musical instruments, bricks and books and ensured the rug and toys were in the shade and reasonably protected from the wind and sun.

Anu took her babies outside and positioned herself between Sophia and Oliver using the cushions to support them just in case they rolled over. She handed Sophia and Oliver a streamer and gently stoked it along the baby's hands and face saying, 'Feel the streamer flutter across your face, is it nice and soft?' Anu reached up and gently swayed the mobiles and wind chimes, creating different sounds as she did so. 'Listen, what can you hear? Can you hear the wind chimes?'

Oliver rolled over and Anu passed him some bells and placed them gently in his hand. Using another set of bells, Anu quietly shook the bells and observed Oliver carefully to see his reaction to the noise. Sophia turned to the sound of the music and Anu passed her a set of bells too.

Anu started to sing a range of nursery rhymes in tune to the sounds of the bells while maintaining eye contact with Sophia and Oliver. Anu carefully tied a set of bells loosely to Sophia's ankles and watched while Sophia lay on her back kicking her legs, enjoying the freedom of open space and the sound of the bells.

Conclusion

With some preparation and planning, Anu was able to take her key babies outside and enjoy a range of activities . Anu made good use of the natural resources, using the trees as shade and also as a way of hanging mobiles, wind chimes and streamers.

When outside, remember to protect babies and young children from all types of weather and all wildlife including insects.

Maintaining quality

- Have defined areas – both small and large. This could include a mark making area and a role-play area.

- With any new resource, show the child how to use it first.

- Provide manoeuvrable equipment which can be moved from one area to another to offer different experiences

- Use all types of surfaces including grass areas, hard areas and muddy areas. Where possible, provide slopes and hills.

- Have suitable storage facilities so children can choose which toys they want to play with.

- Allow the children to take risks within a controlled environment.

- Know your children and their interests through observation and assessment. With a little thought and time, it will be easy to follow and extend their development by introducing various activities whilst outside.

- Watch the children carefully and watch for signs of enjoyment and signs of non-enjoyment. Look out for facial expressions and hand gestures. These are good indications of how the child is feeling.

- Remove and/or repair any broken resources.

- Join in but don't direct – this opportunity is for the child so follow their lead and interests.

- Offer the experience again, and next time add something different to extend the activity.

- Ensure you follow your policies and procedures and that you have taken the necessary steps to ensure the safety of children when outside, for example, putting a cover on the sand pit to prevent animals entering. Do risk assessments on the equipment and provide sun protection for the children on hot summer days.

- After each session, does the area still look inviting and interesting for the next child to experience?

Quality checklist

✓ Is the outdoor environment exciting and inviting?

✓ Have you defined areas within the outdoor space for different types of opportunities, for example, a mark making area and a construction area?

✓ Do you see the outdoor environment as important as the indoor environment?

✓ Do you provide suitable clothing to allow the children to access outdoors in all weathers?

✓ Do you offer free flow both indoors and outdoors?

✓ Do you change the outdoor area frequently offering different experiences and opportunities?

✓ Do you use the local community as a resource and take children on walks around and about your setting?

✓ Do you ensure that all children have access to the outdoor environment on a daily basis?

Links with early learning indicators for under 3s

Play underpins the delivery of all the EYFS. Children must have opportunities to play indoors and outdoors. All early years providers must have access to an outdoor play area which can benefit the children. (Practice Guidance for the EYFS)

Being outdoors has a positive impact on children's sense of well-being and helps all aspects of children's development. (The Learning environment 3.3 EYFS)

Personal, Social and Emotional Development

- Develops a curiosity about things and processes
- Takes pleasure in learning new skills
- Develops confidence in own abilities
- Self-confidence and self-esteem
- Creates and experiments

Communication and Language

- Begins to develop language
- Express themselves through babbling and talking
- Watching and listening to others
- Learns new words and meanings
- Explores and experiments with sounds and words

Physical Development

- Gradually gains control of their whole bodies
- Uses a range of small and large equipment
- Using tools, equipment and materials for particular purposes
- Develop and practice fine motor control and coordination
- Starts to show an awareness of space
- Explores by repeating patterns of play

Construction

Introduction

Construction helps children to improve their motor skills and hand eye coordination. Children enjoy making things and exploring a range of textures including natural materials such as bricks. With many aspects of construction, there doesn't have to be an end product, there are no right or wrong ways and children can explore freely whilst contributing to all aspects of their learning and development.

One of the early construction resources for babies is a set of stacking beakers. They can be used in many ways, such as for building towers, knocking over, tapping to listen to sounds, counting with, hiding things underneath, just to mention a few. Children aged three and over still enjoy playing with stacking beakers and they can be a very cheap resource.

Resources

A good set of bricks can be very expensive but it is definitely worth investing in good quality bricks that will last for years and can be adapted so easily. However, there are other items that can be easily collected to use for construction with very little cost.

- Small/large wooden bricks
- Stacking beakers
- Empty boxes – all sizes
- Empty containers
- Plastic and foam bricks

Extending your resources

- Add small world – a set of animals, dinosaurs or cars.
- Use drape/fabric.
- Listen to music.
- Link to a favourite nursery rhyme/song.
- Have available pens and paper for children to decorate boxes and containers.
- Tool kit.
- Hard hats.

Make sure with all your wooden resources, that they are splinter free and safe to use with children.

Top tip

Make sure there is plenty of space for construction to happen – remove tables and chairs and enjoy playing on the floor.

- Construction is best carried out on the floor or on a flat surface. Try to avoid construction being placed on tables.
- Talk about construction and show children how to build.
- Ensure there are plenty of resources for all the children to access with ease.

- Is it the right construction set for the child's ability and is it challenging?
- Ensure there is plenty of space, especially when large bricks are involved!
- The construction area needs to be available for children to access by themselves.
- Ensure the room is set up to encourage the children to experiment with construction.

Think about the positioning of the area:

- Is it visible?
- Is it accessible to all?
- Does it look interesting and inviting?
- Will it interrupt any other activities that are happening at the same time?

Be creative

Very young babies

- From an early age, babies should have the opportunity to experience many aspects of construction, especially the enjoyment of blocks. Position a very young child on her back on a play mat and build a small tower of fabric bricks next to her. Let her knock them over with her toes or fingers.
- Sit with a baby between your legs and build a tower of soft blocks directly in front of him. Show what happens when you knock them over and use plenty of encouragement and praise when he copies you.

As babies develop

- With slightly older children, watch the children build for themselves. Use different textured bricks for children to build with. Have a basket with resources nearby for children to choose from e.g. small world animals, cars, soft toys or a range of ribbons.

- Encourage a small group of children to build a tower together or decide on certain criteria such as building the tallest tower or building a blue tower. Extend this by collecting a range of the same colour objects from around the environment, provide an empty box, natural materials and a drape – offering the children the chance to explore and construct using a range of textures and materials.

- Collect a range of recycled items such as cartons, plastic tubes, empty plastic bottles (thoroughly cleaned), for children to build with. Add paper, card, pencils, wool and glitter.

- Remember to use the floor for these activities as children will prefer to build on the floor rather than being restricted by a table top. 'What if we were Builders?' (A&C Black/Featherstone) has a wealth of visual materials including photos, pictures, diagrams, posters and a background building site mural that can be projected to cover a whole wall!

Taking it outside

All of the ideas can easily be taken outside but make sure the children are protected from the sun, wind and damp conditions. Be aware of insects and other wildlife in the garden.

Some further ideas:

● Make a den outside using drapes or a pop-up tent and put a range of bricks inside for the children to explore by themselves. Add a torch.

● Build with large bricks under a tree and make a den or a house. Have a picnic lunch in the house or have a range of mark making equipment to decorate the den or house.

● Collect large empty boxes and turn into a bus, a train or an aeroplane. Sing associated songs including 'The Wheels on the Bus', 'Aeroplanes, Aeroplanes' and 'Down at the Station'.

● Use a strong cardboard box for a house for children's favourite toys including dolls and teddies. Add a set of keys and a tea set.

● Remember, if the empty boxes get too wet, show the children what has happened and why it has happened. Remove as necessary.

Involving parents

● Share the child's experiences with parents.

● Display children's construction for parents to see and to gain ideas from.

● Encourage parents to bring in recycled resources from home.

● Take photographs and display for parents to see.

● Show parents that for construction you don't need an expensive brick set – you can utilise many resources from around the home.

Barry the local milkman asked Chris the practitioner if he wanted some light plastic crates that were no longer needed by the milk company. This provided Chris with an idea – to change the defined home corner area in the room for two and three year olds into a builder's yard to develop children's curiosity about construction and role-play.

Chris started his planning and preparation. He asked the older children in the three to five year olds' room to make signs for the builder's yards and started collecting boxes, tubes and containers in a variety of sizes. Chris also asked the parents to save any unwanted boxes. He visited building sites and took photographs of buildings being built, materials and equipment used and made the photographs into a couple of books to share real life experiences with the children.

Finally, Chris collected hard hats, tape measures, tools and clipboards and pens and set about setting up the builder's yard.

Chris built a range of towers, large and small, using the crates and boxes. He displayed the signs the older children had made and put tools, materials and spare boxes into a variety of baskets/trolleys next to the building site.

When the children arrived, Chris sat with them and told them about how the home corner had changed and had become a very exciting builder's yard. Chris took the children over, stood back and observed their reactions as they saw the towers and the new area.

Immediately, the children started knocking over the towers and re-building their own. They explored the baskets, putting on hats and adding new tubes and boxes to their towers and buildings. Chris took photographs of the children exploring and building to use later for a display for parents and for around the builder's yard. Chris sat with the children and showed them how to build, balance and experiment with the area, demonstrating the processes of construction.

Shefali collected a dumper truck and moved the vehicle in between the towers saying 'Beep beep, I'm going under the bridge'. Nick followed Shefali and found a lorry for himself and together they were role-playing with the vehicles between the construction site. Chris collected a range of vehicles for the other children to use.

Chris spoke to parents and shared the children's interest. With their permission, and following the correct health and safety policies, Chris organised a trip to see a local building site.

Conclusion

Chris used some spontaneous resources provided by the milkman and turned them into an exciting and thriving builder's yard, showing how easily you can adapt and change your home corner into something different.

This case study shows how quickly one idea for construction can easily be extended in to another area of play, for example role-play. Chris followed the children's interest by taking a small group of children on a bus and showing them a house being built in the next village.

Maintaining quality

- Provide an inviting and stimulating construction area, in a corner on a flat, carpeted area

- Sit with the children at their level and limit the size of the group in the area.

- Know your children and their interests through observation and assessment. With a little thought and time, it will be easy to follow and extend their development by introducing construction activities linked to their interests.

- Use environmental print, clearly label equipment with names and pictures.

- Have small world play available next to the construction to extend the play.

- Watch the children carefully for signs of enjoyment and signs of non-enjoyment. Look out for facial expressions and hand gestures – these are good indications as to how the child is feeling.

- Remove and/or repair any broken bricks or containers.

- Join in but don't direct. This opportunity is for the child – follow their lead and their interests.

- Act out a favourite story/song with the children using empty boxes to represent parts of the story such as 'The Wheels on the Bus' by David Ellwand.

- Remember there is risk of falling bricks, so follow your policies and procedures and your risk assessments.

- After each session or after each child has experienced the construction area, does it still look inviting and interesting for the next child to experience?

- Offer the experience again, and next time add something different to extend the activity.

Quality checklist

✔ Do we use a full range of construction materials?

✔ Do we encourage children to explore and mix various materials?

✔ Can children transport from one area to another?

✔ Do we offer children construction areas both indoors and outdoors?

✔ Do we show children how to use the materials provided?

✔ Do we take photographs of construction that has taken place?

Links with early learning indicators for under 3s

The physical development of babies and young children must be encouraged through the provision of opportunities for them to be active and interactive and to improve their skills of coordination, control, manipulation and movement. (Practice Guidance for the Early Years Foundation Stage)

Personal, Social and Emotional Development

- Develops a curiosity about things and processes
- Takes pleasure in learning new skills
- Develops confidence in own abilities
- Self-confidence and self-esteem
- Creates and experiments

Communication and Language

- Begins to develop language
- Express themselves through babbling and talking
- Watching and listening to others
- Learns new words and meanings
- Explores and experiments with sounds and words

Physical Development

- Balances blocks to create structures
- Enjoys putting objects in and out of containers
- Using tools, equipment and materials for particular purposes
- Develop and practice fine motor control and coordination
- Explores by repeating patterns of play

Mark making

All children should have the opportunity to mark make. Mark making benefits children's self esteem and achievement as the emphasis is very much on the process rather than the end product. There is usually no right or wrong way but children need to have the freedom to experiment and explore with a variety of textures, materials and resources.

Children are communicating when they mark make and it really begins from a very early age. Babies play with food on their highchair tray and this should be seen as mark making and not with negativity about the mess the baby is making! Mark making allows children to express themselves and children learn best when they are 'doing', using a range of quality resources.

Mark making can be messy with the very young. Clear boundaries need to be set and followed as to what is an acceptable mess and what is not. Practitioners should remember this and allow children to explore, create their own ideas and have the freedom to be imaginative. However, some children may not have the confidence to be creative so take it at the children's individual pace and follow their needs and interests.

Mark making materials are best kept in a trolley, where they can be stored and organised, at the children's height. They should be easy to access and displayed attractively to engage the children's curiosity and interest.

Resources

Many mark making resources are easily found and are relatively inexpensive to buy. Your setting will have a wealth of resources that can be used. For a wealth of ideas on mark making and how to make it a really enjoyable experience see 'Child-Initiated Writing' (AC Black/Featherstone).

A good range of resources for children to have access to include:

- A range of crayons, pens, pencils – different sizes
- Paper – pads, notepads, large sheets of paper
- Paint and various sizes of paintbrushes
- Sand
- Dough

- Water
- Cornflour
- Chalk and chalkboards
- Whiteboards
- Easels
- Wallpaper

Extending your resources

- Add glitter to paint, sand, water and dough.
- Include envelopes, stamps, old diaries in your mark making area.
- Provide clipboards with pads of paper.
- Have available ribbons on sticks to mark make in dancing.
- Add sticks to soil, mud, cornflour or sand.
- Have a portable mark-making toolkit.

Top tip

Don't forget to keep pencils sharpened and lids on pens and felt tips.

Further ideas

- In the home corner: clipboards, diaries, calendars, newspapers, magazines, a variety of pens, pencils, and crayons
- In the construction area: notice boards, note books, clipboards, plans, order forms, a variety of pens, pencils and crayons
- For a post office: old stamps, envelopes, note books, calendars, order forms, diaries, letters, tills, a variety of pens, pencils and crayons
- For a shop: order forms, letters, diaries, clipboards, notices, receipts, catalogues, notice boards, tills, money, a variety of pens, pencils and crayons

- Before you start any mark making, prepared yourself and the children. Children at this age will may make a 'mess' and with certain elements of mark making, it may go everywhere but remember this is how it should be!
- Ensure there is opportunity for mark making in every room. It can be as simple as providing a pot of mark making tools with a variety of different types of paper.

- Think about protective clothing but at the same time this shouldn't be so restrictive that it prevents the children from enjoying the activity. You may need protective clothing too!
- Resources need to be at a suitable safe height, preferably in a mark making trolley or in baskets on the floor where children can easily access them.
- Provide a small number of tools for the children to choose from too much choice can be confusing.
- Ensure the room is set up to encourage the children to explore the opportunity.
  Think about the positioning of the activity.
  - Is it visible?
  - Is it accessible to all?
  - Does it look interesting and inviting?
  - Will it interrupt any other activities that are happening at the same time?
- Immediately wipe up any spillages.
- Get down to the child's level and see what the activity actually looks like from their perspective.

Before introducing cornflour, ensure that you and the child are protected and that you have cleaning materials including towels, water and soap close to hand. Mix cornflour with water until the mixtures goes to a paste. Handle the mixture yourself to ensure it is at the correct consistency.

Starting is as easy as having the child sitting on your lap and pouring a small amount of the mixture into a tray and letting the child play and explore it. Show the child what to do. Put your hands into the mixture too and use plenty of praise and encouragement while experimenting and playing. Make patterns together. If a child doesn't like the texture and feel of the cornflour, reintroduce it at a later date or try putting the cornflour into a zippy bag, seal well and let the child explore the patterns of the cornflour within the constraints of a bag.

Add a drop of food colouring and explore the patterns the mixture now makes. Use warm water when first mixing and offer a different feel and sensation. Extend this by putting cornflour into a shallow low water tray and offering a range of tools to mark make with.

As the child becomes confident with cornflour, extend and develop their interest by having a basket close by with a range of resources including brushes, mixing pallets and small world items. Offer the opportunity for the child to mix the cornflour with water themselves.

Taking it outside

Mark making is easily transferred outside but make sure the children are protected from the sun, wind and damp conditions. Ensure that there is always an area available outside for mark making to take place.

Some further ideas:

- Position a table outside with various mark making materials on it.

- Take a painting easel outside along with a painting trolley containing various resources for the children to use. This can include paintbrushes, objects for printing, paints to mix and glitter.

- Fill a water tray with various materials, for example sand, mud, cornflour or water so children can use their fingers use fingers to mark make. Extend by adding twigs or sticks

- Provide chalks for the children to use on floors, fences and walls. The rain will wash the marks away.

- Create a muddy area for children to explore. Provide welly boots and suitable clothing to protect the children while they walk, jump or touch the mud. Encourage the children to mark make in the mud using sticks and twigs.

- Take a CD player outside. Follow your health and safety policies with electricity and wires outside. Encourage the children to dance and make patterns in the air using streamers and ribbons whilst they dance.

- Cover an area outside with paper and place a range of materials and resources in baskets to encourage mark making.

- Put water in to paint pots and let the children paint outside using water and paintbrushes. Extend by offering a range of resources to use, different sized brushes, various printing materials including sponges and printing objects. Follow on with an actual painting activity involving paint.

- Attach drapes to trees or a piece of secure equipment and make homes, tents or hideaways for the children to explore. Inside, place a range of mark making tools and papers for the children to use.

Involving parents

- Share the child's experiences with parents and show how easily activities can be adapted and enjoyed at home.

- Share with parents the importance and benefits of mark making with food for small babies.

- Take photographs of all kinds of mark making and share with parents.

- Encourage parents to mark make during bath time, using fingers or bath crayons if available.

- Make up small mark making bags for parents to take home and use – include paper, some streamers and pencils.

- Reinforce with parents the importance of the process and not the need to have an end product.

- Ask parents to collect and save any unwanted resources including old diaries, used stamps, old birthday cards, calendars and envelopes.

- Ask parents to involve their child when writing lists or writing letters, for example make a shopping list together or write a letter and then post it in the letter box.

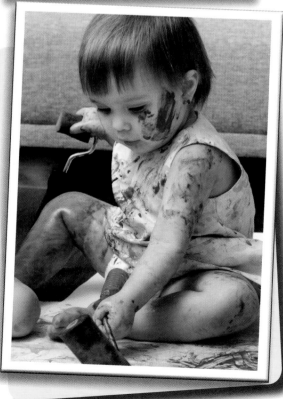

Gaynor is an experienced practitioner leader in the two to three year old's room and it has come to her attention, through observing a new member of staff (Laura), that mark making is not always available for children to access daily while playing outside.

Working closely with the new member of staff, Gaynor re-organised the mark making trolley ensuring that the trolley was attractive, divided into sections and that it included portable writing boxes. The trolley contained paper of all sizes and colours, tubs of pens, felt tips, crayons, pencils, scissors, brushes, sticky tape, envelopes, rulers, clipboards and notebooks. The mark making trolley was then taken outside for Gaynor to be a role model to Laura.

Gaynor and Laura positioned themselves close by the trolley and waited. Two children, Sally and Jessica, walked over to the trolley and started to explore. Both children handled the materials and then picked up the portable writing boxes and took them over to a corner of the outside area. Gaynor and Laura observed and listened to the children from a distance and decided not to join in the activity just yet.

Sally and Jessica emptied their boxes and started mark making on the envelopes. After a few moments, Gaynor walked over and said, 'Are you writing a letter, Sally?' Sally nodded and continued with her writing. Jessica looked over to Sally and copied what she was doing. Gaynor noticed that Sally was beginning to look around and seemed to be losing interest in the activity.

'Shall we make some stamps so we can post the letters? Who are you writing a letter to?' Gaynor asked. Sally turned to Gaynor and replied 'Mummy' and together they made some stamps and then posted the letters in the post box in the home corner.

Conclusion

As an experienced practitioner, Gaynor was able to role model to Laura, the new member of staff, the importance of watching and listening to children and following their lead and interest.

This activity also shows the importance of allowing the children to explore by themselves and only intervene and direct when needed. Gaynor allowed Sally and Jessica to investigate the mark making trolley by themselves and offered direction to extend the learning and the activity.

Maintaining quality

- Work sensitively with children as practitioners play a crucial role in encouraging children to mark make especially with creative materials such as cornflour and mud.

- Ensure that all the materials do work, that pencils are kept sharpened and that lids are put back on pens and felt tips.

- Know your children and their interests through observation and assessment and plan accordingly. With a little thought and time, it will be easy to follow and extend their interests.

- Show the children how to use materials/resources and help them become familiar and confident with them.

- Provide opportunities for children's specific religious or cultural beliefs.

- Watch the children carefully and watch for signs of enjoyment and signs for non-enjoyment. Look out for facial expressions and hand gestures, these are good indications as to how the child is feeling about the activity.

- Join in but don't direct the activity, this opportunity is for the child, follow their lead and their interests.

- At this age, mark making is about the doing, there is no right or wrong way to do this so it is accessible to all.

- Don't over clutter the activity, keep it simple and allow for children to choose what they want.

- Value children's mark making and give praise to develop their self esteem and their sense of achievement.

- Offer the experience again and next time add something different to extend the activity.

- After each session, does it still look inviting and interesting for the next child to experience?

Quality checklist

✓ Do we provide a mark making area in every room?

✓ Do we provide a full range of resources where children can easily access them?

✓ Do we ensure pencils are always sharpened and can be used?

✓ Do we ensure there are enough materials for children to access?

✓ Is mark making available both indoors and outdoors?

✓ Do you share the importance of mark making with parents?

✓ Do you value children's mark making? At this age, there is no right or wrong way to mark make.

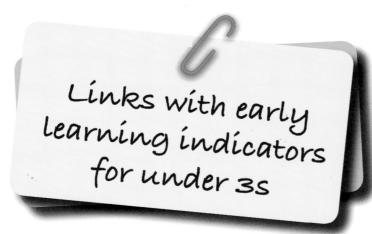

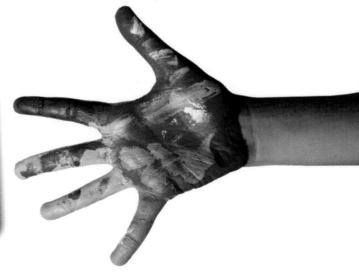

Links with early learning indicators for under 3s

Children will be making marks for a wide range of reasons, each equally valid. Through their marks, they are communicating their ideas, expressing their feelings, developing their imagination and creativity and testing their hypotheses about the world. These opportunities for making thinking visible are fundamental to children's learning and development and should be the entitlement of every child.

(Mark Making Matters National Strategies for Early Years)

Personal, Social and Emotional Development

- Develops a curiosity about things and processes
- Takes pleasure in learning new skills
- Develops confidence in own abilities
- Self-confidence and self-esteem
- Social development including making relationships
- Self-control

Communication and Language

- Express themselves through babbling and talking
- Watching and listening to others
- Learns new words and meanings

Physical Development

- Uses tools, equipment and materials
- Develops and practises fine motor control and coordination
- Body control, poise, balance

Useful books and songs

Babies and young children love books and songs and they provide a perfect way of communicating with the very young.

During any activity, books and songs can easily be included to extend the activity and used to follow children's interests.

A selection of suitable books

Dear Zoo by Rod Campbell (Campbell Books)

Each Peach Pear Plum by Janet and Allan Ahlberg (Penguin Books)

Giraffes Can't Dance by Giles Andreae and Guy Parker-Rees (Orchard Books)

Monkey Puzzle by Julia Donaldson and Alex Scheffler (Campbell Books)

Noisy Farm by Rod Campbell (Campbell Books)

Owl babies by Martin Waddle (Walker Books)

Peace at Last by Jill Murphy (Campbell Books)

The Tiger who Came to Tea by Judith Kerr (Collins Books)

The Very Hungry Caterpillar by Eric Carle (Penguin Books)

Tickle, Tickle by Helen Oxenbury (Walker Books)

We're Going on a Bear Hunt by Michael Rosen and Helen Oxenbury (Walker Books)

Whatever Next by Jill Murphy (Campbell Books)

Who's Hiding under the Sea? by Debbie Tarbett (Little Tiger Press Books)

A selection of suitable songs

Dingle dangle scarecrow

Five currant buns

Five little ducks

Five little monkeys

Head, shoulders, knees and toes

Hokey kokey

I am the music man

I'm a little teapot

If you're happy and you know it

In a cottage in the wood

Incy wincy spider

Miss Polly had a dolly

Old MacDonald had a farm

One finger, one thumb keep moving

Pat-a-cake

Peter hammers with one hammer

Rock-a-bye baby

Round and round the garden

Row, row, row your boat

The farmer's in his den

The wheels on the bus

This little piggy went to market

Tommy Thumb

Twinkle, twinkle little star

Wind the bobbin